Living with Dementia:

A Memoir of Caring for a Parent

Patricia Garrity

Table of Contents

Preface v

Family Tree of Immediate Family and

    Names Used in this Book......................ix

Introduction...xi
"At once they left their nets and followed him."
Matthew 4:20

Chapter 1: Food Habits 1
"'For I was hungry and you gave me food . . .'"
Matthew 25: 35

Chapter 2: Loss of Sight...................................25
". . . for we walk by faith not by sight."
2 Corinthians 5:7

Chapter 3: Heart-to-heart Chats.......................35
"Children, let us love not in word or speech
but in deed and truth." 1 John 3:18

Chapter 4: Confusion..41
"Open my eyes to see clearly the wonders of
your law." Psalm 119:18

Chapter 5: Physical Decline 60

*"'For life is more than food and the body
more than clothing.'" Luke 12:23*

Chapter 6: Dementia during a Pandemic 74

*"'. . . He has sent me to proclaim liberty
to captives . . .'" Luke 4:18*

Chapter 7: Gifts 96

*". . . we even boast of our afflictions, knowing
that affliction produces endurance, and
endurance, proven character, and proven
character, hope . . ." Romans 5:3-4*

Conclusion...115

*"In all circumstances give thanks . . ."
1 Thessalonians 5:18*

Preface

My purpose in writing this book is twofold. One is to write about the development of the disease dementia and how it impacted my mother's life. Mine is not a medical or academic explanation. It is my experience of watching the disease progress in someone with whom I lived. I did not receive much information from medical professionals about what to expect regarding my mother's dementia. I assumed that this was for two reasons. First, I am sure they cannot say for sure what path dementia will take in each person. As I have spoken with others who have a family member with dementia, there has often been some similarity to our experiences yet no two of our experiences are identical. The other reason I think doctors shy away from telling one too much about what to expect is to keep from planting seeds that may or may not come to fruition, and to keep caregivers and family members from jumping to conclusions that may or may not be correct. What I share here is simply what I witnessed.

My other goal in writing this book is to write about how the disease impacted my life. Not about how it inconvenienced me or made my life miserable but about how it made me a better person, at least for the time that I lived with dementia, by stretching me beyond my comfort zone and by reminding me daily of my reliance on God. My hope is to highlight the gift that my mother's dementia was to me. That may sound strange. A gift is something desirable, and I would never desire that someone develop dementia. Yet my time with my mother – and with her dementia – profoundly impacted my life for the good.

The idea of writing a book came from my sister-in-law Colleen. About six months after I moved in to care for my mom, she suggested that I keep a journal to use in writing a self-help book for other caregivers of persons with dementia. I laughed and said the book would never sell because no one would believe what I wrote. Plus, the idea of a self-help book never occurred to me. I did not think that I had anything to offer others about caring for someone with dementia. I just followed the path my mother's disease placed before me each day.

I did not begin keeping a journal until April 2020, approximately six weeks into the shutdown of the Covid-19 pandemic and approximately one month before my mom died. At that time, I began keeping a list entitled, "Mom's events." Part of me wanted to document what was happening with my mom; another part of me wanted a therapeutic outlet where I could write what I was living with and thus experience some relief from stress by expressing it on paper. So, when I decided to begin writing this book, I only had a month's documentation. However, what I also had was almost three years of text message exchanges between Colleen and me and between my sister Maryl and me. After downloading all of them, I spent hours reading through them and highlighting any conversations that had to do with my mom. Those conversations, combined with some strong memories and with my journal entries, led to what follows.

Family tree of immediate family and names used in book

Pat and Ed Garrity

- Daughter Janann, husband Tracy
  - Grandson Zachary
  - Grandson Chico
- Daugher Maryl, husband Larry
  - Granddaughter Bridget, husband Isa
    - Great-grandson Joseph
    - Great-granddaughter Grace
    - Great-granddaughter Caitlyn
  - Grandson Brian, wife Eileen
    - Great-granddaughter Nora
- Son Ed, wife Linda
  - Grandson Jonathan, wife Katya
  - Grandson Colin
- Son Bob
- Daughter Pat
- Son Tom, wife Colleen
  - Grandson Joe, wife Kate
  - Grandson Nathan
  - Grandson Trevor
  - Granddaughter Hannah, husband Matias
  - Grandson Ryan
- Niece Patty

Friend Guillermo and his son Alejandro

Introduction

"At once they left their nets and followed him."

Matthew 4:20

I was 60 when my father died of heart failure at age 93. He died on my parents' 69th wedding anniversary, August 21, during the solar eclipse of 2017. For sure, I will not easily forget the date of his death!

He left behind my mother, age 92 at the time, who had recently been diagnosed with dementia. A doctor's diagnosis was not really necessary – although my brother Ed took her to a neurologist to receive one. Her behavior and memory loss during the previous years had made it clear that something had changed in her. Of course, my father saw the changes more than the rest of us, since he was with her every day. He used to complain that she would take 2 hours in the grocery store. Or that she would stand and stare at open kitchen cabinets for an hour at a time. I thought he was exaggerating.

He died on a Monday, and his funeral was the following Friday. That gave my 5 siblings and me a couple of nights to figure out what the next step would be for our mother. Although she and my father had moved into an apartment in a senior facility, my mother was not in a position to live in that apartment alone.

At some point in our many conversations that week, I said, "I could take medical leave from my job to stay with and care for mom."

My siblings all replied, "You could and would do that?" And that was about the length of the discussion. We all agreed it was the best plan for our mother. And since her health had been worse than my dad's, we also thought several months of leave would be more than enough time – no one expected my mother to live beyond a few months with her health issues and without my dad.

My parents lived in Aurora, Illinois, where I had grown up. Aurora is approximately forty miles west of Chicago, where I had lived and worked most of my adult life. The year before my father died, he and my mother had moved into Fox Knoll Retirement Community – now called Ascension Living Fox Knoll Village. They rented a two-bedroom apartment in the Independent Living section. Rent included breakfast and dinner for them every day. My dad had come to the conclusion that my mom could not and should not cook anymore.

The real attractions Fox Knoll had for my dad were indoor parking in an attached garage and the fact that Fox Knoll was a Catholic organization and, as such, offered Mass and Communion Services throughout the week. When I decided to move in with my mom, I left my job, my condominium home, and the familiarity and independence of my life in Chicago to live with her in a community of senior citizens, most of whom were older than I yet younger than my mom, but all of whom were moving further and further away from being able to live on their own. The people I came to know at Fox Knoll were lovely, even if we were at very different points in our life journeys.

Truth be told, although I still had a job I loved as Principal of Cristo Rey Jesuit High School in Chicago, I was beginning to think a little about what my next step would be after Cristo Rey. Helping my parents had been something I had offered while my father was still alive, telling him to keep me in mind if/when they got to the point of needing help. I do not think my father would have taken me up on my offer while he was alive. My parents were just too stubborn and too independent to consider my leaving my job. But days before my father died, as I visited him in the nursing home where he had gone to regain his strength after a fall, he asked me how I was doing staying in the guest room in their apartment so that my mom would not be alone. I said I was doing fine and added, "Don't make it too comfortable, or I may not leave!" And he said, "I would love that." I took that to mean he wanted me to stay with my mom when he was gone. He knew he was dying.

As has always been my experience, God had plopped in front of me the next step in my life – the "what's next?" after a career I had loved, and the opportunity to honor what I think my father's desire was.

In some ways, I was the least equipped of my family to take on this role with my mom. Being single, I was certainly free of immediate family obligations. Four of my five siblings were married and were parents and thus knew the selflessness necessary for caring for dependents. My brother Bob was a priest and, as such, well equipped with a faith that helped him face any challenge. I was single with no children. My mom used to love to say that I had 500 children, referring to the students at the school where I worked. But those children did not go home with me at night. In reality, the closest I ever came to experiencing a parental role were the two separate times I baby-sat my brother Tom's five children for a week at a time – once so that he and his wife Colleen could take a much-needed vacation, and once so that she could travel with him to a meeting in Europe for the company they owned. Going from zero to five kids overnight was a shock, and the stories of those two weeks have lived on and made us all laugh even to this day. The experience of having to put the children's needs first and of prioritizing their safety above all else, if even for such a brief period, was probably good training for what was to come with my mother.

From mid-August 2017, until her death on May 29, 2020, I was my mother's full-time caregiver. I did so with the incredible moral support and gratitude of my siblings, their spouses, my mom's grand-children, and her great-grandchildren. I could not have done so without the generosity of the faculty and staff of Cristo Rey Jesuit High School who made the necessary adjustments to keep the school moving forward in the absence of a princi-pal until it was clear that I would not be returning to the school. I benefitted from close friends who consistently checked on how I and my mom were doing.

No one could have prepared me for the experience I would have.

Dear God, thank you for the experience

of caring for my mother.

Amen.

Chapter 1

Food Habits

"'For I was hungry and you gave me food . . .'"

Matthew 25: 35

One of the first, very obvious changes in my mother was her ceasing to use soap to wash dishes. She began to rinse and wipe dishes and somehow thought that was good enough. Anyone who knew her – particularly her children and grandchildren – knew how fastidious she had always been. I am not sure if it was a result of her training as a nurse or of her desire as a mother to keep her children germ free, but cleanliness was one of her obsessions. One day some years ago, just to be funny, two of her grandsons actually ate food off her kitchen floor just to prove what they had always said: "Grandma's floor is so clean you could eat off it!"

One time as she was 'washing' the dishes, I commented that she should use soap. She actually engaged in a conversation about this by asking, "Oh, why?" I explained that soap would clean the dishes better than just water and that it would kill germs that might be present on the dishes. At that moment, I had the strangest experience – as if I were outside of my own body, observing the interaction, and thinking, *Where is my mother and what have you done with her?* – an experience I had more times than I can count during my time living with my mom. I cannot say that I never again suggested the use of soap. But I do know that I more often than not began simply taking the dishes she 'washed' out of the drying rack and putting them with the dirty dishes I was going to wash.

For the fastidious woman that she had been, she also developed a practice that was completely counter to her nature. She began reaching into my glass of ice water to pick out ice cubes to chew. She did this when I stepped away from my glass for even the briefest period. If I stepped into my bedroom to look for something, I could hear the rattling of the ice in my glass in the living room where I had left it. More than once I said, "That is my drink, mom. I wish you would not stick your hands in it. I will fix you a glass of water with ice if you would like." Each time she apologized and said she would not do it again. But it was as if she could not control herself, and so of course it would happen again. Something about the crunching of the ice in her mouth seemed to offer her some enjoyment or comfort, but why she was so drawn to taking the ice from my glass rather than having her own I will never know.

This loss of attention to the details of cleanliness was part of a larger decline in her ability to do all the things she had done in the kitchen for so many years. Our house was a full house when I was growing up! My five siblings and I, my mom and my dad, and my paternal grandfather all lived together. Occasionally another young person in crisis also stayed with us for a while. For three meals a day – that included lunch because we went home from school for lunch in those days – my mother made sure there was enough for each of us to eat his fill. Dinner often included the addition of my maternal grandmother who was a widow and lived nearby. And although the hosting of Thanksgiving and Christmas dinners alternated between my mom and her sister-in-law, my Aunt

Virginia, one of those holidays each year would have my mom preparing dinner for a crowd of roughly thirty people.

Food was my mother's modus operandi of offering care to others. If someone had a death in the family, my mother was the first to prepare a meal and deliver it. If someone was sick, homemade soup was soon on the doorstep. If one of her children got the flu, a light meal would be ready as soon as the person could tolerate it. Daily, her care for my father while he was alive was expressed through her cooking.

So, no longer being able to function in the kitchen and express care in the way she always had done was incredibly difficult. It was probably more difficult to watch than for her to experience because she never really gave up thinking she could cook as she once had. The saying "old habits die hard" does not come close to expressing the impossibility of my mom's turning off the tapes in her head that said, *What can I fix you to eat?*

I learned that my dad was not kidding when he told me that my mom had started to open the kitchen cabinets and stare at the contents for forty-five minutes or more. I did not think that was possible. Until I witnessed it, time and time again. Often, I would find water all over the floor in front of the refrigerator from her staring into it for long periods, either because she was trying to figure out what to prepare or because she was using the light of the refrigerator in place of the ceiling light in the kitchen. At first I thought the refrigerator was failing. I soon realized that no defrost or dehumidifying function could work for that long without causing extreme condensation or melting. Since my mom could not judge the passing of time well anymore, she had no idea how long

6

she was keeping the refrigerator open. I tried to explain to her what was happening with it. She could not understand, so I simply began closing it as often as I could when I found it open.

I must admit that the food issues presented me the greatest challenge of living with my mom. Maybe that was because I had lived alone for almost 40 years with control over what I ate and when. Maybe it was because it was so painful to see my mother lose the ability to do something that gave her such joy for so long. I am not sure. But I do know that the things I feel worst about when I look back over the nearly three years I cared for my mom tend to be the arguments we had about food and about cooking. And what makes me feel bad is that I allowed myself to argue with her, a woman deep into dementia who could not help what was happening to her brain. One blessing of dementia is that my mom quickly forgot our arguments.

I stewed in guilt feelings afterwards; she, as was the case for so many parts of her life, could not remember the incidents shortly after they happened. If I have learned anything from living with someone with dementia, it is the fact that one can choose how to respond to situations. I did not have to argue with my mom; I chose to and could have chosen different responses. At my best moments, with God's help, that is what I was able to do.

There were times when I thought I had to speak up for her safety and that of others in the building. Like the first time she left a potholder touching one of the electric burners she thought she had turned off. I commented that she was not to use the stove if I was not there. She got angry and insisted she had never done that before with a potholder. I simply pointed out that now she had.

On another occasion, she raised her voice, something she did not do often, in response to my telling her she should only cook when I was there because of safety reasons. She asked what safety reasons. I pointed out a few recent incidents which I thought were unsafe. One was when she heated store bought cookies in the oven on the plastic tray on which they came. Luckily, I discovered them before the plastic had completely melted. She screamed that she would not be criticized, that she had been married 70 years and had never caused a fire. I asked her what she would say if she heard that similar incidents had happened in another's apartment in the building. She said she would tell them they have to be careful. I told her that was what I was doing.

When I was particularly concerned that she would use the stove in my absence, I began flipping the circuit breaker when I left so that the electric stove would not work. The first time she discovered what I had done, she told me she thought my action was disrespectful. I reiterated my concern for safety and insisted I did not mean to be disrespectful. With time, she stopped attempting to use the stove as much, and she appeared to have forgotten that I might be turning off the circuit breaker. I do not think that she realized the safety concern she presented in the kitchen. I think the progression of her disease caused her to be able to do so little that even turning on the stove seemed like a task out of her capability.

My brother-in-law Larry even tried to convince her not to turn on the stove. He is a retired fire fighter and worried greatly due to the things he had seen that one serious mishap in the kitchen could have grave results for the entire Independent Living community. One evening when my mom and I were at his house for dinner, he prefaced his conversation with her by stating that in all the years that he had been a part of our family, he had never asked my mother for anything. He then proceeded to ask her for one thing: to stop using the stove. She agreed to do so but then stewed about it for a couple of days because she knew she didn't plan to stop but did not want to be caught in a lie to her son-in-law. She also wondered who had told him about her dangers in the kitchen. She asked me to drive her to his house so that she could clarify things by telling him that she could not say for sure that she would no longer use the stove.

Sometimes, I was able to indulge her. Like the time I came back from swimming laps to find that she had prepared me a sandwich for lunch with what I am sure was some meat near or beyond its expiration date. For some reason that day, I was able to thank her and eat what she had prepared. I did not enjoy the taste of the food, but I was glad to have avoided an argument with her and hoped that my accepting the sandwich helped her to feel productive in some small way.

Many persons view grocery shopping as a necessary evil, or, at best, an essential task. My mother came to view grocery shopping as one of her absolute favorite outings. It wasn't really about making necessary purchases, although our needing some items certainly made the trips more meaningful. It was about browsing the aisles, touching products, and attempting to read labels.

Her preferred store was a small retailer named Prisco's. It was a family-owned store, and my mother loved their employees. My mom was always one to support small businesses. When we were growing up, she shopped at Buy Rite, a small store in the neighborhood that she preferred over the larger grocery chains. As small stores go, Prisco's was at the top of the list because of their incredible array of in-store prepared food: pizzas, meatloaf, lasagna, and ham salad were just a few that my mom loved to buy. And while I liked the store too, I had to really work hard to demonstrate the patience necessary to allow my mom to enjoy the outing.

In the beginning of my time with her, she was able to browse the aisles more or less on her own. I remember the day I told her I would be right back and went to the sports bar next door to have a beer. I tried calling my sister-in-law Colleen in New Hampshire, hoping she would enjoy a beer at her end while we chatted. There was no answer. So, I texted her daughter, Hannah, who was living in South America at the time. There was no answer from her either. So, I drank my beer, used the bathroom, which was one of the reasons I orig-inally went to the place to start with, and went back to Prisco's to find my mom less than halfway through the store. During those early trips to the store, my mom would browse many aisles – produce, deli, meat, canned goods, and ice cream. With time, she was lucky to get through produce, deli, and meat. Eventually, she had to wait in the car while I shopped because she was just too worn out to go in.

I also learned that my dad was not kidding when he said it took my mom 2 hours to get through the store. Once, I asked her if she could please agree to be done within 45 minutes because we had somewhere to go. She insisted that she could never spend even that long in the store! I reminded her a normal trip took approximately an hour and a half. She didn't believe me and was shocked when I told her 45 minutes was up and that we needed to leave. My dad used to drop her off at the door of the store and park and take a nap in his car while she shopped. Maybe that is where I got the idea to go have a beer while she shopped. My leaving her alone in the store did not continue for long. I started to worry that she would not feel well or become disoriented and not know what to do. Once when she wanted me to drop her off on her own, I asked her what would happen if she had one of the incidents where her legs didn't work. She told me she would ask the butcher for help. The next time I was in the store alone and one of the employees asked how my mom was, I told her that story. She agreed that of course the butcher would help my mother, if necessary. My mom was right. The employees of Prisco's were very nice people.

We often had arguments about what she should buy. Out of habit, she always wanted to buy milk. Neither she nor I drank milk, and neither of us used it in coffee. But she thought she needed to have milk on hand for whoever might stop by. Quart after quart of milk went bad before anyone used it. Or as the expiration date approached, she would ask me repeatedly who I thought could use it to avoid it being wasted. Every once in a while, I was able to convince her to wait to buy milk until we knew someone was coming to visit, or to buy a pint rather than a quart or gallon so that the waste would be less. The other thing she insisted upon buying was meat for her to cook. Since I was trying to convince her not to cook, I tried steering her away from buying stew meat for her oven stew or ground beef for her meatloaf, neither of which she was capable of preparing well anymore.

In fact, nothing she prepared was good anymore. This was incredibly sad to witness since she had prepared such large quantities of food for all of us for so many years. One of the ways she and I did use ground beef was to make chili every few weeks. She always wanted to help but could not figure out how to use the various can openers

I had bought for her ease of use, even after repeated demonstrations. Once as we were eating on our TV trays, as we usually did, I found something crunchy towards the bottom of my bowl of chili. She explained that she thought the chili was a little too watery so threw in some uncooked brown rice just before serving. Knowing how long brown rice takes to cook, I stopped eating it right then, fearing what it would do to my stomach uncooked.

Some of the concoctions that she came up with were mindboggling. Like the time I came home to two dishes she had made. One was noodles to which she had added pumpkin seeds and tortilla strips that came with a chopped salad kit. She thought they were noodles, too. The other dish was black eyed peas, onions, tomatoes, celery, and potatoes cooked together to which she added beef broth and brown sugar. When I pointed out the pumpkin seeds, she began to pick them out. I stated that she should not try to remove them on my account, and that I was not going to eat the dish anyway. She could not understand why, told me it was good, and proceeded to freeze it for another time. Or the time she pulled from the refrigerator a 'soup' she had made. It consisted of a can of tomatoes mixed with a can of green beans and some uncooked pasta. She then had added that mixture to some delicious home-made split pea soup that my niece Bridget had made.

The old habit of cooking for my dad all those years after their children were grown would simply not die. I cannot even count the number of evenings she would ask me what she should cook for dinner. Many of those evenings, she had no intention of eating herself, since she had snacked on and off all day. One time, I told her not to consider cooking if she was not hungry. But, because I said that, she decided she would eat something. That was not the result I had hoped for. I had hoped she would decide not to think about cooking since she wasn't hungry. Another time, I took the conversation a step further and asked what I thought was a rhetorical question, asking why would she feel the need to cook for me, a woman who had lived on her own and taken care of herself for 40+ years. She could tell by my voice that I was upset and asked why I was yelling. Of course, I could not tell her that I was yelling because I wished we would never talk about food again. I told her she was right, that there was no reason for me to yell. Her answer to my question about why she thought she had to cook for me was as simple and sweet as it could be. She did so because she liked me. That was the closest she had ever come to verbalizing what I probably knew my entire life: my mother expressed love through food and through her interest in attending to physical needs such as hunger and tiredness. Her asking what to cook was an old tape in her head that could not be turned off. My job became to head her off at the pass and cook something before she could begin.

Sometimes, that was nearly impossible. As her sleeping habits got worse, her cooking habits became a way to fill the void of the night. Once, she put ribs in a pan sometime in the middle of the night and let them sit out. With my assistance in turning on the oven, she put them in. My fear was that they had already been spoiled from sitting out too long. She got mad when I asked her what time she took out the ribs. She said she had been cooking her whole life and had never spoiled food. She also added vegetables to the ribs which would all cook for hours. I suggested that the vegetables would be better going in later so that they did not become mush. There not a chance that she was changing what she had planned.

After a few more cross words were exchanged between us, she screamed that she was leaving and going home. All I could think was, *Shame on me*. On another occasion, she put left-over rotisserie chicken in a dish and set it in the microwave but forgot about it. Once again, I had no idea how long it had been unrefrigerated so convinced her we needed to throw it out to be safe. I think the only reason she agreed to do so was because she was sure that someone else had forgotten about it in the microwave.

It was not just the quality of cooking that became a challenge for her. I remember watching her trying to put clean silverware away. She couldn't remember where it went and tried several cabinets, then just stood there for a bit until she remembered the drawer they were to go in. I also remember the time I found a sheet of aluminum foil folded and hung on the rack where the kitchen towel went. I was grateful I found it before she attempted to dry her hands on the towel. That foil would have ripped open her thin, paper-like skin. And I remember the sadness I felt when she, who had always loved her morning coffee, asked me how the coffee could get from the pot into her cup.

In November of 2018, I was scheduled for a routine colonoscopy. Since my mother had never had one, I was not surprised that she was not familiar with the preparation for the procedure. But because she had been a nurse when she met and married my dad, I assumed the nurse in her would honor whatever I told her was 'medically' necessary. I was wrong. She could not understand the required liquid diet the day before the procedure. She kept offering me food, and I kept saying I could not have it. One food item that was allowed was yellow Jello. When I went to eat it,

I found that sometime during the night she had consumed almost all of it. She had forgotten that it was all part of my prep, felt bad about eating it, and proceeded to mix up vanilla pudding as a replacement, with no comprehension that the pudding could not substitute for the Jello. I was not angry. I was sad to think of how many simple things this intelligent woman could no longer understand.

One day about a year before she died, just when I thought she was going to get into her pajamas, she pulled a number of items out of the refrigerator. She wanted to cook some chicken. I put it in the oven. She tried to put a plate of some other food in there and dropped it. I felt angry but kept it to myself. I did tell her that she had had a bad day and wondered why she insisted upon doing things knowing that. I think she realized something was very wrong and was testing herself. She failed the test, I think.

Dear God, thank you for my mother's

selfless example of always wanting

to serve others.

Amen.

Chapter 2

Loss of Sight

". . . for we walk by faith not by sight."

2 Corinthians 5:7

Because this is not a technical or scientific book about dementia, I cannot say for sure that loss of sight is part of the disease. I am not an expert on dementia; I know what I know from observation and experience. I can say that as my mom's dementia progressed, so too, her vision deterioriated.

My mother had been a voracious reader her whole life. She loved reading books, but I do not remember her reading light novels. I remember her reading informative books, such as a biography of Abraham Lincoln which appeared to be about 1,000 pages long. This was back in the 60s, long before electronic readers existed, so I have to think that the hardcover book was also extremely heavy. She also felt obligated to be informed by reading at least 2 newspapers each day: the local *Aurora Beacon News* and the *Wall Street Journal*. Each night before sleeping, she would prop herself up with pillows in her bed and begin reading the two publications. She rarely got through them both before she fell asleep. The remaining parts she would read the next morning, propped up once again and drinking coffee in bed. It never ceased to amaze me how much she could contribute to conversations based on what she had read in the *Wall Street Journal*.

At age 50, my mom returned to graduate school to earn a master's degree in Pastoral Studies, an interest she developed through her volunteer work developing ministries for the elderly in her parish. Books and learning were part of the identity of this educated woman.

When she stopped being able to read, I am not sure. It happened before my dad died. But the effects of this loss were something I witnessed all through the years I lived with her.

She would often complain that her glasses were just not right. When she first said this to me, I made an appointment and took her to the optometrist. I learned what had transpired at her previous appointment: that the doctor had recommended bifocals but that my mom was afraid to try them for fear of not being able to adjust to them and increasing her chance of falling. So, my mom had ordered just reading glasses. During this new appointment, the doctor had reiterated that she needed glasses for both close up and distance and suggested she get a separate pair of glasses for distance. He instructed her to use the distance glasses for watching TV. He also very politely said that if the glasses did not help there was nothing else he could suggest for her.

And thus began the recurrent conversations about her vision and her battle with her two sets of glasses. She could not remember which pair was for distance and which pair was for reading. Honestly, the only reading she was doing at this point was looking at catalogues, focusing on the pictures and struggling to make sense of the writing. I would try to help her select the correct pair of glasses for the appropriate activity, but she still could not see. She would ask to return to the optometrist. I would politely remind her what the doctor had said about not being able to do more, but she would not remember. I would remind her again and tell her that was why we were not going to make an appointment.

What became noticeably clear to me was that her inability to see well and to read was not only due to her vision. It was due to her brain's loss of ability to process the information it was seeing. This, I was sure, was part of the dementia. Often, as my mother was trying to figure out the changes she was experiencing, she would ask me if I thought she had suffered a stroke at some point. I asked my brother Ed, the doctor, at one point, if he thought it would be alright for me to use the word 'dementia' in my answers to my mom. He thought it would be if I used it gently. A gentle approach was not what my dad had taken near the end of his life. When my mom would ask him if she had had a stroke, he would answer, "No, Pat, your mind is demented." That sounded so much harsher than anything I might say with the word 'dementia' in it. I learned to answer my mom's question about a stroke by saying that she had gone to a neurologist with Ed and that a brain scan had shown some changes, a form of dementia, that she had not had a stroke, and that her loss of ability to read was, in my opinion, related to the changes in her brain. That made sense to her. She was relieved to know she had not had a stroke. As it is for many elderly persons, my mom's greatest fear was to have a stroke and live in a vegetative state.

Whether or not these are truly related to her loss of vision or not, I associate two behavior changes in my mom with the loss. The first was her need to touch everything in the refrigerator. In my mind, I compared this to that of a child playing in a sand-box, moving around the toys, and digging with the shovels, basically just enjoying a hands-on activity. Often, I would find her in the kitchen with everything from the refrigerator spread out on the counter. It was her way of taking stock of leftovers and figuring out what food items needed to be used soon. But because she could not see the items well, and because futzing in the kitchen had always been her thing, she would open each container and handle the contents, sometimes combining items from several containers into one, sometimes combining items into some concoction she wanted to cook, always leaving me less than interested in eating anything from the refrigerator because she had touched it all. One time I brought leftover ribs home from dinner with friends, thinking she and I could enjoy them the following night for dinner. The leftovers included ¾ of a slab of ribs, most of a baked potato, and a small loaf of bread. By the middle of the next afternoon, she had handled everything in the container, cutting the potato into pieces, slicing the bread, and eating the sauce off the top of the ribs.

The other behavior change that I associate with her loss of vision is the practice of watching muted TV. I quickly adjusted to this change because the volume at which she would need the sound on the TV because of her loss of hearing and refusal to get hearing aids was excruciating to my ears. But the fact that she did not need the sound to enjoy whatever pleasure she got from watching TV was, in my opinion, just one more example of how the vision loss was really a loss of processing abil-ity. Even with the sound, her brain could no lon-ger process what she was seeing and hearing on the screen. So, we watched hours and hours of muted TV every day. It's a shame that we had to pay for cable when there were only four channels that we watched: The Weather Channel, HGTV, the Food Network, and Fox News, my mother's preferred news source. We watched the weather to start each day. I was most interested in the local weather for the day; my mother was most concerned with whatever bad weather she saw, because she could not distinguish between forecasts in other parts of the country or the world, and forecasts for us in Aurora, Illinois. She loved *Fixer Upper* – she thought Chip was always such a cheerful person – and *The Property Brothers* on HGTV. If she didn't see Chip and Joanna or the brothers for a few days, she worried that they had been replaced by some other show. My mother was always fiercely loyal. She always looked forward to *The Pioneer Woman* on the Food Network, especially when numerous episodes were shown back-to-back. And she thought Guy Fieri was hilarious and laughed out loud repeatedly as she watched him on *Diners, Drive-Ins, and Dives*. During lighter moments of watching Fox News, she would comment on how much she thought Hannity looked like my dad. During more serious moments, she would see bits of reports and piece together in her mind what she thought the reality was. It is difficult to argue with that version of a person's reality.

Dear God, help me always to walk by faith.

Amen.

Chapter 3

Heart-to-heart Chats

"Children, let us love not in word or speech

but in deed and truth."

1 John 3:18

This is a short chapter. My mother was never one to speak openly about her deepest emotions. We all knew her opinions about what she thought was right and wrong. But how she actually felt about things and people was another story. I always assumed that she expressed her emotions to my father. Now when she spoke from the heart, mostly about something related to her decline from dementia, I was there.

Here are the closest things to conversations about her feelings that we had.

A recurrent one was when she would ask me if she had suffered a stroke. I knew she was fearful that the answer was yes. I would reply that no she had not but that her brain had started working differently than it previously had.

There were times after I helped her clean up from a particularly bad bathroom episode that she would say she did not know what she would do without me. I told her she did not have to worry, that I was there to stay and that my job was to help her. I knew that was her expression of gratitude.

This was similar to a particular statement she made several times in the last months of her life.

She would tell me it was time for her to move to Assisted Living and for me to get on with my life. I would answer that I was living my life, that I was not going anywhere until she made her next move which would be to heaven, and that she was getting more attention from me because I lived with her than she would ever get in Assisted Living. She always accepted that answer. I understood that to mean she really did not want to go to Assisted Living. I probably should have spoken about when she would go to God rather than to heaven in reference to her death, since I know I was not in a position to say for sure that she would go straight to heaven. Honestly, that would have fit better with my mother's beliefs about herself – she would never have thought herself worthy enough to go straight to heaven.

Twice my mom confessed to episodes of nervousness. The first was related to her fears for my brother Tom who had chronic health issues as a result of his battle with lymphoma and to her confusion about where she was after waking from a nap. The second was several weeks before she died. She offered no explanation for that one. What she called 'nervousness' I considered possible panic attacks. A quick search on Google confirmed that it is common for persons with dementia to experience panic attacks. I know not to believe everything I read on Google, but at times when I saw what was happening with my mom but did not have a medical explanation for it, I must admit relief at finding information that meshed with my experience.

I remember only three times that my mother referred to her dying. The first was when my sister Janann was visiting in January 2019, in honor of what would have been my father's birthday. My mom commented to us both that she thought she was dying. I was not sure how she felt about dying, but I simply responded by saying, "Well don't worry. Nan and I are both here." The second time was in October 2019. She and I were at The Pancake House when she again said she thought she was dying. Her concern was what I would do when I was finished being with her. I confirmed that I would be done with her when she went to heaven, and that I planned to move back into my apartment in Chicago and that Ed would move out – my brother Ed had been staying in my apartment during the time I lived with my mother. The third was on May 25, 2020, the night she fell and broke her hip. I was with her in the Emergency Room when they informed us that they had a room available for her but that I could not accompany her past the ER due to Covid-19. My mom begged me not to leave her and said, "I'm not going to make it." I kissed her on the forehead and said, "Let them get you comfortable in a room (she was still in excruciating pain) and I'll see you tomorrow." I knew I would not be able to see her tomorrow either but felt I needed to offer her some hope that she would not be alone for long. Thankfully, she was not completely alone the next day because my brother Bob the priest and my brother Ed the doctor both got permission to visit her, one for a pastoral visit, the other for a medical visit.

Finally, there was the time she answered my frustration about her desire to cook with the statement that she wanted to cook for me because she liked me. I took that to mean she loved me.

For my mother, actions always spoke louder than words.

Dear God, help me to live my faith

both in word and in action.

Amen.

Chapter 4

Confusion

"Open my eyes to see clearly the

wonders of your law."

Psalm 119:18

Confusion is an inevitable part of dementia, I am sure. What surprised me was the extent and the variety of my mother's confusion.

I remember the first time that it was obvious to me that she did not know who I was. It was November 21, 2018. We were at The Pancake House for lunch when she asked me if we had invited Pooh, a nickname I received as a child and never outgrew. I told her that I was Pooh, and she looked at me as if I were speaking a foreign language. Several days later, on the 25th, a similar episode occurred but lasted much longer. She became angry because she thought I was one of her two daughters named Patty (she did not have two daughters named Patty – she had one named Patty and a niece that she helped raise named Patty), but not Pooh and not her caregiver. I tried to assure her that I was the Patty who was both Pooh and her caregiver. She got even more upset because she understood that three people had told her they were Patty/Pooh. We stood face-to-face in the kitchen for approximately fifteen minutes while I tried to help her understand. I called my sister Maryl, since we were supposed to be going to her house for dinner, to say I did not know what to do. She suggested that I say we were going to see Grace, her great-granddaughter, who would be at Maryl's. I tried that and a couple of other ways to distract her with no luck. Finally, the fog of confusion cleared – I do not know how – and we were on our way to Maryl's. With time, I got used to the moments when she did not know who I was. Once when she did not recognize me, I laughed when both Bridget and Guillermo suggested that I should have left the apartment and come back in so that she may have recognized me. But the initial episodes made me so sad for her and so fearful of what was to come.

There were times when she thought I was my dad. This was clear when she called me by his name. It was a little less clear when she offered me foods my dad liked. Once, she offered me sardines. I politely declined and said that I did not like sardines. She answered, "You used to like them," and I knew who she thought I was. What was sad about these situations is that it appeared she did not remember that my dad had died. I expected this at first when my dad's death was recent. It was no surprise when she told me one morning that she had spent most of the night looking for my dad. She said she even looked in the linen closet. I laughed with her about that and commented that he did not even know what a linen closet was because she had always taken care of things around the house. But it did surprise me that her forgetting that my dad had died persisted, or should I say popped up, every once in a while. Once, mid-week, she told me she planned to cook a turkey breast for my dad the following Sunday. I suggested that she would not be cooking for dad, since he would not be there.

On another occasion, she fixed a plate of dinner for him. I told her it was just she and I for dinner. She kept asking where he had gone, insisting that he had taken her to the grocery store that day. I said that he was in heaven and that I had taken her to the store. She continued to wonder where he was and looked for his cell phone number to call him. She told me I acted like I knew he died and wanted to know how I knew. I showed her the announcement of his death that had been posted throughout the building after he had died. She did not believe it. She asked me to call my brother Bob to see if he knew where my dad was, but Bob didn't answer. I suggested she get into her pajamas and go to bed, but she said she couldn't until she knew where he was. When Bob returned our call, he said Edward was with her spiritually but that he had died with her and all of us around him. She insisted she had been with him that day. I tried to tell her that her mind was playing tricks on her. Before I could tell her I understood that she missed him, her mind had jumped to thinking he had died that day, alone, and she wanted to know who had told Maryl and Tom and everybody else. I tried to get her to go to bed, but she was too worked up. She next asked if Patty Purcell knew her uncle was dead. I said yes but that it was too late to call Patty to talk about it. Finally, sometime after 10:00p.m., she calmed down enough, probably from sheer exhaustion, to go to bed.

Most of the time, she did remember that my dad had died. But she had no memory of his wake and funeral. She often told me she had not been at either. I assured her that she had stood for the entire five-hour wake, which had been scheduled only to last for three hours, and had greeted every person. I tried to refresh her memory about the lovely funeral Mass that Bob celebrated, or about the family gathering at Maryl's afterwards. I thought she would be happy to know that she paid for the fried chicken we had ordered from Jewel that day so that Maryl did not have to cook. None of it rang a bell. But she seemed glad to know that it all went well.

Sometimes, I just had to laugh about some of the confusion regarding people, both dead and alive. There was the time she told me that she could not remember the name of the other Patty. Or the time that I had to convince her that my mother had not died. Or the time we were heading out to the funeral of a woman we both had known for many years and she asked me if we were to pick up the woman. If I did not see the humor in these, I would have been in big trouble.

The idea of serving food to people who were not present was a recurrent theme. Many evenings, as we prepared to have dinner, she would ask me how many places she should set. I would answer, "Two, it's just you and I, and how about we eat on the TV trays?" something we did almost every single night. There were slight variations to this theme. Sometimes she would pull food out from the refrigerator and set it on the counter and say, "They can just all help themselves," or, "Here is food for any of the boys." Other times, she would augment her question about how many would be there for dinner and ask, "How many of the boys will be here?" I never knew exactly who was included in her reference to "the boys." I assumed she meant her sons, perhaps also sons-in-law, grand-sons, great-grandson, Guillermo, and Alejandro.

Whether my mother was seeing persons that were not there or just recalling memories was not always clear to me. Once, about a year before she died, she picked up a little vase with some artificial flowers in it to throw it out. I asked her why she was doing that, reminding her that Patty Purcell had bought those for her about a year ear-lier so that she would never have to water them and worry about their dying. She insisted that she received them as a gift when she was in eighth grade. Around that same time, on one of our trips to The Pancake House, she commented to me about a couple that walked in carrying a cage with a chicken in it. Of course, there was no such thing. Shortly before Christmas in 2019, she wanted to send a poinsettia to her mom, who had been dead for twenty-five years, but said she did not have her address. When I told her that her mother was in heaven, she was shocked to find out that her mother had died. Her mom was 90, I believe, when she died. If she were still alive, she would have been approximately 115 years old! A couple of months later, in a phone conversation with her grandson Joe, she commented that she was doing well on crutches after surgery. Since she had not had surgery of any sort, I could only conclude that she was confusing herself with Patty Purcell who had broken an ankle and had surgery a year earlier. My mom had started wearing two pairs of underwear – a nylon pair over her Depends. Whenever I tried to suggest that she only needed the Depends, she told me that her grandmother had told her to wear two pairs. One of the times it was clear she was not seeing what was real, was when she asked me where I thought she should put the picture of Tom and Colleen and their kids. She was referring to a refrigerator magnet from Belknap House, a non-profit shelter for homeless families, to which Colleen is very committed. On the magnet was a stick figure insignia of a family.

Holidays, especially during the last year of her life, presented serious challenges for my mother. First, she loved to celebrate any holiday. When we were kids and went home from school every day for lunch, my mom would have a treat for us on even the most insignificant of special days. On St.

Patrick's Day, we would be treated to Shamrock Shakes from McDonald's. On Valentine's Day, we would receive candy or some other little gift. My mom's favorite way to celebrate Labor Day was with a big sundae from Dairy Queen on its last day of business for the season. Now one of the challenges was for her to know even what day it was or whether or not it was a holiday. On Labor Day 2018, she told me she had woken up early but saw no good reason to be up on that first day of the year so had gone back to bed. Was she thinking about Labor Day as the unofficial first day of fall? I had no idea. The greater challenge for my mom was to forget about all the holidays that she cooked huge meals for large numbers of people, something she had not done for years. Her brain could not erase the tapes of all the work that went in to preparing Thanksgiving din-ner or Christmas breakfast after midnight Mass or Easter brunch. But her brain also could not keep straight the dates or days of the week. One evening in November of 2019, three weeks before Thanksgiving, she wanted to cook green beans and potatoes for Thanksgiving dinner. I told her we could cook them and eat them but that they would not last until Thanksgiving. She was not convinced that it was not Thanksgiving and sat up well past her normal bedtime waiting for the company to come. The next morning, she asked me how Maryl's Thanksgiving celebration was. I reminded her it was not yet Thanksgiving. She still did not seem convinced. Several days before Christmas that same year, I worked hard to help her understand that a huge crowd was not coming that day or any day for Christmas, and that we would be celebrating at Bridget and Isa's.

The worst was Easter of 2020. Because it was during the Covid-19 pandemic, there not going to be a family gathering of any sort. Visitors were still not allowed in Fox Knoll, large gatherings of any sort were prohibited, and going into others' homes was not yet recommended. None of that stopped my mom from obsessing about Easter dinner. She saw some chairs on a TV show and wondered if we could borrow those because we did not have enough. And she wondered what time we should eat that would be good for everyone. I just kept saying, "It's just you and I. We can eat anytime you want."

What was most shocking about my mom's confusion as her dementia worsened – even more than her forgetting within a couple of hours that we had gone to Mass that day – was her forgetting how to do some of the simplest tasks. My mom had always been a big coffee drinker. She and my dad were years ahead of everyone else when they prepared their coffee at night and plugged it into an electric timer so that it would be ready when they got up in the morning. So it was particularly surprising to me when I had to explain to her, more than a year after I had moved in with her, that our pot with the built in timer (the same model of coffee pot she had used for years), went on automatically so she did not have to do anything in the morning. When she asked me how the coffee got from the pot to her cup, I showed her. I could not comprehend that she knew how to pour her coffee the previous day but had lost the process overnight.

Around that same time, I washed her favorite cloth purse. It was her favorite precisely because it was washable. When it was dry, she forgot how to put things back into it and tried to stuff everything into her wallet. The day she forgot how to get to the Podiatrist's office in the building where we lived, I was not surprised because she only saw him every couple of months. It was later that day when

she forgot how to get into the car that I was surprised. Instead of putting one of her legs in first,
she attempted to put her head in first but then
could not figure out how to get her legs in. I was
glad to help her, thinking it was just a pause in her
memory causing her the confusion. But when we
went out to lunch and she ordered a hamburger
and just stared at it, I knew she had also forgotten
how to eat such a meal. With my assistance in
cutting the burger and telling her to pick up half of
it with her hands, she was able to enjoy it. More
than once, I found her standing in her bedroom
when she was ready to take a shower. Thinking
the closet was the shower, she could not figure
out how to enter it. Sometimes, she completely
forgot where the bathroom was in our small apartment and headed out the apartment door to go to
it. There were days that she could not remember
how to flush the toilet or to turn off the shower
or where the refrigerator was. The day I took her

to get a state ID, the gentleman taking the picture politely said several times, "No smile and no teeth showing." My mom could not do that. She thought he was kidding; he thought she was kidding. I finally just told her to close her mouth, and he quickly snapped the picture. It always made me incredibly sad to see her not be able to do the simplest of things.

It was even sadder to witness her forget key facts about her own children. One morning in early January 2019, she told me she had gotten confused during the night and asked me if Ed had died. Since her husband and a son were both named Ed, and because I knew she sometimes got confused as to whether or not her husband had died, I clarified, "Do you mean your son Ed?" She said yes, and I assured her that he had not died. The fact that she could not remember whether he was dead or alive was particularly surprising because he had just visited the previous day. It was even more surprising the day she asked me if Maryl had children. She generally saw Maryl several times a week and regularly asked about – and often saw – Maryl's kids and grandkids, all of whom she loved dearly.

Once when she had an upcoming appointment with her cardiologist, she asked me twice how she could call my dad so that he could call her cardiologist to say she could not make her appointment. Why she thought she needed to cancel I was not sure. I said she could not call my dad and that she did not have to worry because her appointment was not scheduled until a few days later. She continued to try to call her cardiologist's office. At that point she rarely initiated phone calls anymore. She did not get an answer. She must have been dialing a wrong number or misdialing the correct number. She then called her primary care doctor's office to ask for the cardiologist's number. I assured her every appointment of hers was on the calendar so that if she had any doubt she could look there. When she had an upcoming appointment with her dentist, she confused the days of the week, took medication she was supposed to take one hour before her appointment, and proceeded to wander around Fox Knoll looking for someone. It was never clear for whom she was looking. I think it was probably I because I had stepped out to take a walk. She never said that, however. It must have been painfully difficult for her to be so confused that she did not know the day or how to use the phone or how to check the calendar for her appointments.

As I said, sometimes I just had to laugh about the stories her mind told her. Like the time I heard her talking on the phone with her cousin Merilyn. It was painful to hear how confused she was about details. She told Merilyn, as she had told others, that the national board of Jesuits told me to go take care of my mother. That was not how it was. I took a leave, basically quitting my job, and Jesuits on the national level had no idea about it. Most did not even know who I was. In the same conversation with her cousin, she said that she was doing better and that she thought I should go back to work.

I have heard many people question the confusion or memory loss they observe in their aging parents, worried that their loved ones are developing Alzheimer's Disease or dementia. And I have read a number of times that confusion and memory loss are related to the aging process. I now know there is an observable difference between what comes with normal aging and what comes with dementia.

Dear God, thank you for my mother's continued pleasantness even as her confusion worsened.

Amen.

Chapter 5

Physical Decline

"'For life is more than food and the body more

than clothing.'"

Luke 12:23

My mom's death certificate gives her cause of death as, "Senile degeneration of brain." In other words, she died from dementia. Yes, she had a traumatic fall and shattered her hip days before she died. But the thing that actually caused her death was the disease that caused her brain to die slowly and to lose its ability to communicate with and control her body as it once had. Again, this is not a scientific or medical explanation; this is simply what I observed as I accompanied my mother during her last years.

Her physical decline was equally as painful to watch as her mental decline. Approximately eight months after my dad died, my brother Tom called my mom on a Saturday morning, as had been his custom for some years. That particular Saturday, my mom had an exceedingly difficult time talking on the phone, especially with the enunciation of words. A year or so before my father died, my mother had a toxic reaction to a medication that caused her to have extreme difficulty speaking due to a condition called tardive dyskinesia. But her speech had improved significantly once the medication was stopped. So her difficulty that day was unexpected. After their conversation, Tom expressed to his wife Colleen his sadness at realizing that his mother could barely talk on the phone anymore. Her ability on the phone improved somewhat at times but truly never returned to what it had been. Perhaps this was from the tardive dyskinesia. Or perhaps dementia was robbing her of one more thing.

Within a few days after that, she had two separate episodes of not being able to move her legs. Both times she was standing in the kitchen and called for my help. I sat her on her walker and wheeled her to her chair in the living room. Both episodes looked to me to be times when there was a disconnect between her brain and her legs. Her doctor suggested I take her to the Emergency Room for an evaluation because the movement issue was new. After several hours of tests and waiting for results, the ER doctor told us that there was nothing new to explain her difficulty moving. In my layman's mind, I chalked up the episodes as just part of the worsening of her dementia. No one told me that. I just figured it out for myself. Because the difficulty with her legs was not permanent, I also concluded that this was just how it was going to be with her illness, that some days would just be worse than others.

The good thing about that particular trip to the ER was that the results of a urinalysis were negative for infection. This was significant because that was the first time in two months, after multiple rounds of three different antibiotics, that she did not have an infection. She had urinary tract infections (UTI's) so frequently that I got really good at knowing the symptoms, doing a home test, and calling her doctor for medication. She, like many elderly persons, did not demonstrate the normal symptoms of a UTI. The only symptom she displayed was confusion. And because she was already confused from having dementia, it was sometimes difficult to know whether the confusion was from an infection or not. As I used to say to the nurse at her doctor's office, "Goofy on top of goofy is hard to distinguish."

There were plenty of times when she just did not feel well. She often complained of dizziness and thought it was caused by one of her medications, although her doctors did not think so. It was more likely that it was caused by dehydration, although I tried my best to keep her drinking fluids. Sometimes she was too tired to do anything, especially after one of her many nights of not sleeping well. It is not uncommon for people with dementia to have disrupted sleep patterns and to confuse days and nights. I think this happened with my mom because she began to complain almost daily that she had not slept the previous night. However, I could not confirm this was happening because any time I was up after she had gone to bed she appeared to be sleeping. I must admit, though, that her sleep did not appear to be restful. She made all kinds of noises while she slept. She moaned, she yelled, she hummed, she talked, she sang. I had to sleep with a noise machine in my room to drown out the sounds that would have otherwise kept me up all night. At times, her breathing was a bit labored, and her coloring was not good. I attributed these 'bad days' to her generally slowing down physically. The unfortunate thing was that when she did not feel well, she missed some family get-togethers which, under normal circumstances, she would have been thrilled to attend, celebrations such as Easter brunch and her great-grandson's eighteenth birthday dinner. After one get-together that she forced herself to attend, even though she was exhausted, I made the profound comment to my sister-in-law Colleen, "If it kills her, then she will be dead."

As the time passed, my mom began to have diffi-culty swallowing. This was most evident in the fre-quency with which she would aspirate something as she ate. Whether it happened at home or in a restaurant, an incident of aspiration could lead to long periods of coughing. My fear was that she would develop pneumonia from the aspiration. I am grateful that never happened. Her doctor sug-gested that she drink with a straw. She tried it a few times but did not stick with it. Using it was just something to which she could not adjust. I tried to be careful about what we ate at home, choos-ing dishes that had a good consistency for her to swallow and that did not contain seeds of any sort. That did not help much. I knew there were thickeners that could help with liquids. She did not even consider trying them. Looking back, I am glad that she kept such a good appetite right up until the end that altering the texture of her food

just seemed like it would interfere with her enjoyment of eating.

There were some foods I had to eliminate for her.
One was Twizzlers Pull-n-Peel cherry candy. I used
to buy large bags and treat her and me to some of
it many afternoons. When she started choking on
it, I stopped offering it to her. I hid it in my car and
splurged on it when I was driving without her in the
car. It made me laugh to think I was eating behind
her back! Another change I made during her last
year was to remove any non-essential pills from
her daily medications. I consulted her doctor to be
sure it was alright to remove her over-the-counter
supplements and her osteoporosis prescription.
The goal was to decrease the number of pills she
had to take, which were getting more difficult for
her to swallow, while maintaining those essential
for her heart and thyroid functions. This helped

immensely, and she seemed relieved each morning to see so few pills that she had to take.

My mom's skin was very delicate, as I am sure is the case with many elderly people. Hers was made even more fragile from a lack of use of lotion to help keep it supple and from her use of a blood thinner. When she was on Coumadin, the slightest of bumps resulted in wounds that were huge and deep. The bleeding could last for days or even weeks. This was when my father was still alive. He was the one who patched her up, using his skill as a former surgeon. When she switched to Eliquis, the wounds and bleeding were far fewer but not nonexistent. Once, she and I went to get our nails done. Her manicure took less time than my pedicure, and I had asked her to remain seated where she was until I was finished. She insisted upon coming over to sit with me. So, one of the nail technicians helped my mom to her walker and wheeled her over to me. Unfortunately, as my mom moved to the walker, she bumped her leg on a screw and proceeded to bleed rather heavily. The young lady felt awful and got a bandage for my mom. I tried to assure the employee that she had done nothing wrong, that my mom's skin was so fragile that accidents like that often happened to her. I made up my mind right then that if I took my mom for another manicure, I would insist that she remain seated until I could help her. I did not want anyone else feeling responsible for her wounds and bumps. Another wound she got on her shin was from her bumping the edge of the coffee table near her chair in the living room. I discovered this one morning when I found her asleep in her chair surrounded by blood all over the carpeting. That wound lasted for weeks and required a daily change of bandage. Still it got infected. Her circulation to that part of her leg was just not as good as it once was, so her body was not able to help the wound on its own. She asked me to please not tell anyone about how she cut her leg. I was not sure why. Perhaps she was afraid some family members would jump to the conclusion that she was not safe in her own living room. Because I had my own doubts about her ability to be safe, I told her that I could not promise that I would not tell anyone because my job was not only to care for her but also to keep the family informed about her and about her health. She seemed to accept that. With oral and topical antibiotics from her doctor and with daily wound care, the injury eventually healed.

During the last year of her life, she fell five times. Each of these falls scared me because I so feared a bad injury for her. I knew that many elderly do not survive too long after breaking a hip. It was also painful to recognize with her that her balance was not good and that her body was just giving out. Four of the five falls did not involve any serious injuries, even the time when I had to call an ambulance because I was afraid she had broken her hip or seriously injured her head, both of which she had hit when she fell. Thankfully, everything checked out fine that time. Normally, she would be stiff for a few days after a fall. Once she bruised her back from hitting the windowsill and experienced pain for a couple of weeks when she lay on the bruised area. Twice she woke me by using the alarm system I had bought for just such occurrences. The receiver was in my bedroom, and she pressed the button hung around her neck to sound it. One of those times, I was able to get her up on my own. The other time, in the middle of the night, I had to call the Fire Department for assistance because I was afraid

I was going to injure myself in attempting to get her up. The final awful fall resulted in a broken hip for which an ambulance and hospitalization were necessary. She died four days later.

A month before she took that final fall, I was texting with my sister-in-law Colleen, offering sympathy for the fact that she and my brother Tom were about to drive north from their house in Florida to their house in New Hampshire. Because of the Covid-19 pandemic, and because of Tom's health issues, they had planned to drive the approximately twenty-two hours straight through so that they did not risk catching the virus by stopping at a hotel. She told me she thought their drive seemed easy compared to my upcoming month of May, with my mom's growing weakness and the continued Covid lockdown. I told her I would be surprised if my mom lasted through the month of

May. She was surprised and asked why I thought that. I guess I just saw the writing on the wall from observing my mom's decline.

Dear God, help me to be free

from earthly attachments.

Amen.

Chapter 6

Dementia during a Pandemic

"'. . . He has sent me to proclaim liberty

to captives . . .'"

Luke 4:18

March of 2020 began the shutdown of much of life due to the Covid-19 pandemic. The date that life changed so dramatically is etched into my brain: Friday, March 13. I remember it as the last day that schools throughout Illinois had regular classes. I felt so bad for my great-nephew Joseph and his sister Grace, both of whom were high school students, and for the students at the high school where I had worked previously. Little did I know the impact the shutdown would have on a person with dementia.

Before Covid-19, my mother and I followed a weekly routine, when she was up to it. This was driven first and foremost by her desire to attend church services. Fox Knoll, where we lived, had Mass or Communion Services on Monday, Wednesday, and Friday, and Mass for Sunday was offered late afternoon on Saturday. On Tuesdays and Thursdays, we would go to late afternoon Mass at McAuley Manor, a nursing home and rehabilitation center not far from Fox Knoll. The rest of each day revolved around our plans to attend these services. Many days included lunch at The Pancake House, a restaurant she loved, which is approximately a block away from Fox Knoll. She loved the food at The Pancake House, for sure. But even more so, she loved the people who worked there. The owner Jesús called her, "Mamá," and opened the door of the restaurant for her when he saw us pull up and park. His son, Uriel, was a gentleman like his father and treated my mother with the utmost respect. The waitresses Tiffany and Meagan treated my mother – and me – like we were family. My niece Bridget and her children, my sister Maryl, and my cousin Patty often came to 4:00p.m. Mass on Saturday and then came to my mom's apartment for snacks and a drink. Early on during my time with my mom, their visits sometimes included dinner, but even visiting for that long eventually became too much for my mom. Many days, my mom and I went to the grocery store just to browse, but always coming away with some purchase. A haircut or manicure was added every few weeks. With a visit by my brother Ed, usually on the weekend, to see my mom and to bring me my mail from Chicago, the routine of the week was complete. That is until Covid hit and every part of her routine was gone.

All church services were canceled. Every restaurant was closed for in-person dining. Grocery stores remained open but not recommended for the elderly who were most at risk of dying from Covid, and particularly for elderly persons like my mom who lived in a retirement facility because of the risk of spreading the virus to even more vulnerable seniors. Visitors were no longer allowed at Fox Knoll. The life my mother had come to know no longer existed.

Very early in the shutdown, the challenges for my mom were predictable. Her memory was so poor that she could not remember from day to day that we could not go to church or out to lunch or that she could not go into the grocery store. By six weeks into the shutdown, I noticed my mother's confusion growing exponentially.

Late one afternoon in April, she stood up as if to leave. When I asked her where she was going, she said to Holy Angels, her former parish, to pick up a box of food for the poor. I stated that such an event was not happening that day. She got agitated and said it was, that she had signed up to do this weekly. When I again said there was nothing like this scheduled, she told me I did not make any sense. She then asked for my car keys. I told her she no longer drove and that my car is a stick shift anyway; she said she could figure it out. I tried to ignore what she was saying and help her watch TV. She then insisted that I get going and go by myself to Holy Angels. When I told her I was not going, she said, angrily, "Edward, I have never seen you act like this." She obviously thought I was my father.

Two days later she saw something about Joe Biden on the news and commented that she had worked with him for the 8 years that he was Vice President and that he was a nice guy.

The next morning when I gave her a cookie to have with her coffee, which was her daily routine, she commented how good it was and told me that my mother had brought those cookies from Chicago. Twice, she then reached as if to pick up something from the floor – there was nothing there. It was not clear to me what she was seeing.

Later that day, I was participating in a webinar in my bedroom when I heard her talking in the kitchen. Thinking she was speaking to me, I went to ask what she was saying. She pointed to her empty walker and said she was speaking to them, telling them to be quiet as they go down the hall to the left.

One recurrent theme for my mom was that of little children in multi-color outfits. Frequently, when

I would open the shade in the living room, she would comment, "There go the little children in their multi-color outfits! I can't believe they are riding their bikes into the river!" or, "There they go! I can't believe they are swimming in the river in the middle of winter!" One day as we were driving home from Maryl's house, she yelled several times for me to stop or be careful. When I asked why, she said, "Because of the little children in their multi-color outfits that are on the road!" She was angry that I did not stop, and she thought the girl leading them was very irresponsible to take them out on a busy road right into traffic. I assured her I would be cautious and not hit children on the road.

One day in early May, as we talked about what we would have for dinner, my mom wondered where "the boys" (her sons) were and what they would each have for dinner. I explained to her that Bob was in Naples, Florida and would cook for himself or get carry-outs; Tom was in Niceville, Florida and would have dinner with Colleen; Ed was in my apartment and would cook or get carry-outs. She felt better knowing this!

If there was a positive to being locked down for Covid, it was that food from the dining room of Fox Knoll had to be delivered to residents' apartments to prevent large group gatherings in the dining room. She had stopped going to meals after my dad died. But if she liked the sound of the menu for the day, we would accept the food being delivered. This helped in two ways: we did not have to discuss what we were going to fix for dinner, and she was taking advantage of some of the meals that she was paying for in her monthly rent.

The next morning after getting dressed with my help, my mom stated that she was not doing very

81

well. Some hours later, she told me she thought she should go to live in Assisted Living. I told her that she was staying right here, that I was her 'assisted living'. She then asked if I thought she should go home. She had asked me this before. And I was never quite sure how to answer it. I had no idea what 'home' she was thinking of. That day, I just said, "No, I don't think so." My usual response was that she and I were staying there until she goes to heaven. Maybe that day I should have said, "Yes," giving her permission to go to heaven, if that is the home she was thinking of.

My mother loved it when my brother Bob came to visit from Florida. She loved his visits for many reasons, one of the biggest being that he is a priest and so could celebrate Mass for her in her apartment every day. One morning when I woke up, and not during one of Bob's visits since he could not come because of the pandemic, my mom had moved all of his Mass items plus a nail file over to the table. She was asleep in her chair, so rather than asking her what she planned to do with those items, I just put them back on the bookshelf where they had been. The following morning, all those items were back on the table. When I asked her what she was planning to do with them, she told me she was going to return them to the Deacon, to whom they belonged. I told her they were Bob's and suggested I put them back on the shelf. She told me she was so glad I was able to remind her to whom they belonged before she gave them away. I asked her why the nail file and little scissors were among the items. She said that the Deacon had a really bad hang nail that he needed to take care of.

She then told me how glad she was to see me, which I found interesting since we were together day in and day out! When I asked why, she said because no one else was up yet that morning!

As I helped her get into bed that night, she asked me where Grace (one of her great-granddaughters) was going to sleep. I told her at her house.

There were times when it was obvious that my mother did not know who I was. It was very obvious to me one morning, but I was not sure who she thought I was. Our morning routine had been to drink coffee and watch the Weather Channel muted until we would see the local weather. I would give her a bowl with her morning pills – the bowl was to catch any that she dropped – and another with a banana and a cookie. I would drink coffee until I was ready to eat something after a while. That morning, as was often the case, when I came to the living room, she was asleep in her blue chair. When she woke, I was reading on my Kindle, which I had done most mornings. She asked me if I was doing schoolwork – a sure sign that she did not know who I was since I no longer had schoolwork, either as a student or as a pro-fessional. I said no, I was reading. She asked me what I was reading. I said a book, and that was good enough for her. She then asked me if I liked cereal for breakfast – something I had eaten maybe once in the 2 ½ years in which I had been living with her. I said, "Not usually." She then asked if I wanted toast. I said, "No thank you, not right now." She commented that I could turn on the sound of the TV if I wanted. Since we watched most TV muted, I knew this was another sign that she thought I was someone other than the per-son who was a part of these routines day in and day out – her daughter. Next, she asked if I liked the new school system (I assumed she meant e-learning because of Covid-19.) I said I really didn't have anything to do with a school system anymore but wished the kids could be in classes because I thought it was better for them. If I had to guess, I would say that she thought I was my niece Bridget who is a teacher.

I went for a walk that day and returned around 11:30a.m. She knew then who I was but wondered where our guest had gone. When I asked what guest, she said, "The one that spent the night with us." I said it was just the two of us. She said he knew just what to do and had brought her pills to her that morning. I said that was I. She said he didn't want oatmeal. I didn't respond. She questioned whether she had given enough thought process to our guest. I said she did fine because it was just the two of us. When I opened my computer to type something, she said he was a little guy who knew everything about computers.

One afternoon in mid-May, I opened the shades so we could see the green grass and the river. She must have asked me 5 times if I saw all the children in their multi-color outfits in the river. I tried not to answer, but she insisted. So, I simply said, "I'm not seeing what you are looking at. Isn't the grass beautiful?"

The previous night, I had gotten out of the shower around 8:00 and found her standing in her room fully dressed with her winter jacket on. I asked her where she was going. She wasn't sure but wanted to know if there was a Mass "that morning" that we could go to. I told her no, all public Masses were still canceled, and that it was nighttime and time for her to get into her pajamas. She proceeded to sit as she was in her living room chair. She asked if I had slept well. I said I hadn't slept yet, that it was night. It took a few reminders before she seemed to grasp it. She then laughed a little and said that both Pattys had asked her where she was going.

A little later I told her it was time to put her nightgown on and that I would help her. As I tried to convince her to get into her bed, she expressed great concern for the flowers. (There were 3 beautiful bouquets of flowers in vases in the living room; she had received them from Tom, Bob, and Janann for Mother's Day.) She was worried because she said they had all been taken out of the vases and were going to stain the couch. I assured her several times that they were all secure in vases and fine. She finally lay down and went to sleep. I remember wishing there were something I could have done to relieve her anxiety!

One dark, rainy morning, I woke a little after 7:00a.m. After checking on my mom who was sleeping in her blue chair in the living room, I took the luxury of going back to bed. At 9:00, a neighbor knocked on my bedroom door – inside the apartment – to let me know that she had found my mom wandering the hall in her pajamas. My mom had her pillow and the green blanket from her living room chair on her walker. When I asked her where she was going, she first said, "To the records room." I had no idea what that meant but wondered if it was from her work as a nurse 70 years ago. A little bit later she said she was going to the other living room that she and Patty used. She could not understand why Verna, the neighbor, had brought her home. I told her that there was nowhere she could go right now because of the pandemic except to walk the hallway for exercise but reminded her that she did that when she was dressed. She did not understand.

Late the next afternoon, I returned from doing an errand. My mom asked me when my dad would be back. Before I answered, she remembered that he had died. So, I thought she got it. But then she said she wanted to call him and didn't have a phone number for him. I said she didn't need one – that she could just talk to him or pray to him directly since he is in heaven.

May 17 was my mom's 95th birthday! The previous day she had commented that the washcloth on the counter near the bathroom sink was clean even though it was wet. I asked her why it was wet. She said she had rinsed it out. I am quite sure that meant she used it for something – maybe just to rinse her face – so that it was not 100% clean. It is not the first time she had told me this. Another time when she told me the same thing and I asked the same thing, she said that the washcloth had fallen into the sink, so she had rinsed it. Again, I am sure the washcloth was not filthy but don't know that I would have called it clean – and neither would she have in her earlier years! As she prepared to take a shower on her birthday, I told her I was taking her dirty clothes from her laundry basket so that I could wash them. She said,

"Oh, you don't even have to use soap!" I said, "I'm washing them, of course I will use soap!" She asked, "Isn't hot water enough?" I said no. That this was from someone for whom cleanliness had been next to Godliness was unimaginable.

After Verna had found my mom wandering the hall, I purchased a door alarm for our apartment. I was glad to know that it served its purpose the day it sounded at 6:15a.m. as she opened the apartment door. I jumped out of bed to find her in her pajamas opening the door and planning to head somewhere. When I asked where, she said she was going to check on everyone. I assumed that meant family members because as I led her back to her bed she whispered, as if trying not to wake anyone up.

A week later we celebrated Memorial Day with burgers from the Bristol Tap on Maryl and Larry's patio. I had picked up the burgers after Maryl and I had visited my dad's grave which is right down the road from the Tap. Truth be told, we prayed and asked my dad to please put in a good word with God for our mother, who appeared to be failing in many ways. Even though my mother had been to the Bristol Tap numerous times, she claimed she had never eaten a burger from there and that the one she ate that evening was the best she had ever had. She fell in the garage that night as she used her walker to move from my car to the building entrance, a routine we had done every day for almost three years. I knew from witnessing the fall that it was a bad one. I first called Maryl, who said she would be there quickly. I then called Ed who was the Health Care Power of Attorney for my mom. He and I had worked together for months to keep my mom from the emergency room for two reasons: 1) the usual 'fire drill' of tests to be done in the ER seemed a bit like overkill since my mother had expressed that no matter what, she did not want to have another surgery or extraordinary treatment of any kind; and 2) the protocol up until that point of the pandemic had been that no one could enter the ER with a patient, and we did not want her to be alone in the hospital. But this fall was different. I told Ed I was sure she had broken something and that I needed to call an ambulance. He agreed. Some hours later, when I was allowed into the Emergency Room to see her – I was thankful that the protocols for Covid had changed slightly - I learned that my mother had broken her hip, would need surgery to repair it, and would have to be admitted to the hospital where visitors were not allowed. That was Monday evening, May 25. On Tuesday, Ed consulted with my siblings and me to make sure we all agreed that it was not in our mother's best interest to consider surgery to repair her shattered hip. We knew she did not want more surgery, we doubted that she could survive the surgery in her already very fragile state, and the success of rehab if she did survive surgery was unlikely. We all agreed to provide comfort care for her. On Wednesday, she was moved from the hospital to Maryl and Larry's house with hospice care. We did this so that her children and grandchildren and great-grandchildren could see her, with appropriate Covid precautions, since visitors were not yet allowed at Fox Knoll. We will all be forever grateful to Maryl and Larry for opening their home for this to happen. On Friday morning, she died with a number of family members at her side. The date was May 29. It happened to be Maryl and Larry's wedding anniversary. My father's dying on my parents' wedding anniversary guaranteed that I would not forget the date of his death. My mother's dying on Maryl and Larry's anniversary guaranteed I would not forget the date of her death.

My mother did not die from Covid, but I believe that Covid certainly contributed to her death. She was 95 with dementia, so her death was not unanticipated. But the shutdown most certainly contributed to her rapid decline during those months. During one of Dr. Philip Moore's last home visits to my mom, long before the pandemic, I told him that my mother's confusion was getting worse and asked if he had any suggestions. He said that the best thing I could do was to keep her in a routine. That's what I did until Covid-19 struck. The cessation of everything that had become routine, I am sure, hastened my mother's death.

Dear God, comfort the families of so many

elderly who were alone during the pandemic.

Amen.

Chapter 7

Gifts

". . . we even boast of our afflictions, knowing

that affliction produces endurance, and

endurance, proven character, and proven

character, hope . . ."

Romans 5:3-4

People everywhere could not have been kinder to me when they heard I lived with and cared for my mother. Many had elderly parents themselves so could relate to the difficulties my mother was facing. Others had careers they could not imagine leaving. Still others had strained relationships with their mothers, I think, and thus could not bear the thought of living with them.

On this last note, I think I was a fairly typical female growing up who had issues with her mother at many points. When I was young, it was because she would not let me see certain movies or wear clothes that did not meet her approval. Or she had the nerve to be interested in how my day at school went when she knew I hated school and never wanted to talk about it once the day was done. As I got older, it was because she was not incredibly open to hearing others' opinions about politics or social justice issues. It drove me crazy that even suggesting another side to an issue – even if it was not something I believed – was really not accepted. Looking back, I now under-stand that these were my mother's ways of doing what she thought was right to fulfill her role in teaching me and my siblings. And my bucking up against her was the process of my developing into an independent person. It now seems ironic to me that the person from whom I was establishing my independence ultimately became completely dependent on me.

While I appreciated the many comments of, "Wow, I don't think I could do that," or, "Take care of yourself – the work you are doing can take a toll on your health," I honestly felt blessed to be able to do this for my mom, even in the most frustrating moments. So, I would respond, "I am happy to do it!" and meant it.

I have always believed that good things can come from bad things. I would never have wished lymphoma on my brother Tom, but his illness led him to spend more time with his family and to sell his business earlier than he dreamed he would but for top dollar. My friend Casey's husband's horrific accident and resulting brain injury have caused her to relish any semi-normal moments for her and her daughter while she learns ways to provide comfort, love, and support for her husband in ways that are new to her. The untimely death of Katie's husband has made her even more available and dedicated to her career as a school counselor. I should clarify that I believe good things can come from bad, and it is the gift of eyes of faith that allow us to see those goods.

I did my absolute best to care for my mother during her last years. I fear, though, that I may have gained more than she did from the experience. The 'bad' – her dementia – led me to receive 'goods' I never could have predicted.

Many elderly, and particularly the elderly with dementia, become incontinent. Incontinence can be of the urinary tract or of the bowel or both. My mother experienced both. Part of her problem was age combined with numerous pregnancies – she had six children. As one of her doctors said, "It's a problem of age and plumbing, and the fix is probably not something you want to do at this point." The other part of the problem was dementia. As I watched my mother's worsening incontinence, I came to understand that her brain no longer communicated with the rest of her body as it once had. By the time her brain knew she had to go to the bathroom, it was too late. That was my very unacademic interpretation of what was happening. To spare you the details and to protect my mother's dignity, I will not expound upon the topic. Use your imagination to picture the worst. Even in those worst moments, I saw a good. Somehow, I was able to keep myself from being sick as I cleaned up. That lesson of mind over matter will remain with me. And somehow I was able to set aside my own needs at the time and completely focus on her needs at the moment. I often compared my caring for my mother to the role of a mother taking care of a baby. One major difference was that babies grow to be more independent; my mother was growing to be less independent. Since I had never had children of my own, I could only imagine what a mom feels when, time and time again, she has to put her child's needs before her own. I had just a small taste of such opportunities for selflessness while caring for my mom, but I know I am a better person for having experienced it.

At the same time, I also learned even more than I already knew about the importance of self-care. I never felt guilty about scheduling a time each day for exercise, even the time when I returned to find my mom had fallen. I knew that my presence may not have prevented her fall and that the stress relief I received from exercise made me better able to care for her. In her better days, I looked forward to a Friday or Saturday night when, once she was settled in front of the TV or in her bed, I

could go to the theater to see a movie or go to the
Paramount Theater to see a musical or a concert.
Sometimes guilty feelings would tug at my heart
as I left her, feeling bad that she would be alone
for a couple of hours. But I knew that a little time
away for me, doing something that did not focus
on her, was good for the two of us in the long run.
Approximately once a month, I would go across
the street and treat myself to an Asian massage
at the old-house-converted-to-a-business with
the sign that said, "Asian Massage." My friends
laughed when they heard I was a regular there.
I found the no-frills place to be perfect, offering
an excellent massage at almost half the price
of a salon, performed by Chinese women who
did not speak English, and since I do not speak
any Chinese language, silence during the massage was thus guaranteed. I took almost every
chance I got to have dinner with friends. My mom
often got more excited than I, both to hear about

whatever restaurant I went to or to sample its left-overs and to know that I was keeping in touch with friends that I had known since grade school. Two of my friends, Casey and Beth, both had elderly mothers, so our dinners became a form of therapy for us all. My mom, never being one to think of herself, supported me in each of these activities of self-care, although I doubt she could have labeled them as such. When family members took turns to stay with my mom so that I could spend a few days in Des Moines, Iowa, visiting my friend Guillermo and his son Alejandro, my mom often wanted me to stay with her and whichever of her children was staying with her. It was not that she did not want me to visit Guillermo. She simply did not want me to miss anything fun that might transpire with her and my sibling. The thought that I could use a break never really occurred to her. Self-care was not a part of her vocabulary, but she always wanted everyone in her family to have fun. I learned the importance of regular self-care in order to be able to do my job for her, that self-care and the ability to put another's needs before one's own go hand in hand.

The lesson of mind over matter applied to other aspects of my life with her, beyond dealing with her bathroom issues. I learned that how I responded to a situation was a choice. I could choose to demonstrate patience, even if that is not what I felt. I learned this lesson the hard way – by not demonstrating patience at times and realizing how terribly unkind that was to a woman who could not help the condition in which she found herself. I remember a time she said to me, "Well you don't have to be so crabby." And I realized she was right. No matter what I felt, I did not need to demonstrate crabbiness to her. In fact, the best way for me to respond to her was to say whatever was good for her to hear. Just as I did when I told her repeatedly that she was not going to Assisted Living. I did not deny that her health was such that she needed assistance; I assured her I was there with her until the end. She and I both knew her health was not going to improve, so there was no point in saying anything that suggested it may. I believe it was more important for her to hear that even as bad as her health was, she would not be alone. This was a great way for me to be reminded that most of the time it was not about my feelings; it was about what my mother needed to hear. And I could choose what she would hear from me. I cannot say I applied this lesson perfectly all the time; I can say that I knew it in my head and in my heart and tried really hard to practice it with my mouth. I prayed every day for God's help to do so.

In fact, she set the best example for me of choosing how to respond to situations. My mother chose to be joyful, no matter how bad her situation got.

She and I were both fortunate that her dementia did not cause her to be nasty or violent. But in the end, it was still her choice how she responded to her challenges. And she did so joyfully.

She was also a great example of a person who knew her priorities. This fact was evident every day when she first decided what time we would go to Mass or Communion Service. That was the thing that was most important for her, and she never wavered from it. She and my father had gone to daily Mass for years, so keeping the practice alive was also a part of my mom's keeping part of her identity alive. Daily prayer had been a part of my life for quite a while. With my mom I had the luxury to follow her lead in planning our days around prayer. Even now I remember my mom and her example each time that I set a priority for prayer time.

One of the gifts I received from going to Mass or Communion Service with my mom every day was that of getting to know some men I consider holy: Deacon Jack Roder of Fox Knoll; Msgr. Bob Wilhite of the Diocese of Rockford; Abbot Vincent Bataille, Abbot John Brahill, Fr. Charles Reichenbacher, Fr. Joel Rippinger, Fr. Nathanael Roberts, and Fr. Paul Weberg, all Benedictines of Marmion Abbey. Their attention to my mother, and to me, their senses of humor and positive views of life, and their abilities to bring Scripture to life were inspirational. I am grateful for my interactions with them.

When friends consult me as they consider job changes, I often comment that going out when one is still playing his/her A game is the way to do it. I felt that was the way I left my job as a school administrator. I still loved the mission of the school. I was fortunate to work with incredible colleagues and families. I think I was still effective in my job. I felt like a bigwig in many ways. I held a key leadership position in a nationally recognized school. I was fulfilling my desire to make a difference in the world by being part of a Catholic institution that served low-income Latino students exclusively. I traveled several times a year to visit other schools or to gather with my counterparts from other similar schools. And without giving it too much thought, I chose to walk away from that in order to take care of my mom and live with her in a retirement community. Overnight, my responsibilities shifted from what seemed like huge decisions about how best to educate the children of immigrants and help them achieve the life they dreamed of in the United States to what could have seemed like rather mundane decisions of what to have for dinner or where to go for a ride. I have to say I never missed those bigger decisions. My mother's complete dependence on me quickly gave me a sense of humility. If she through aging and dementia and the loss of my father had given up any ability to do things independently, who was I to think that the things I was doing to help her were anything less than the work I had been doing? I cannot say that I was not aware of the fact that my world had been diminished in some ways by my choosing to live with my mom. I can say that the diminishment just did not seem as important as the work I was doing for my mom. I was humbled to be able to do what I was doing. It was, perhaps, the first time in my life that I had understood the principle of Ignatian Indifference. Whether it was by impacting hundreds of students and their families or by offering assistance to my mother, I could serve God. My brother Bob told me I was like the disciples in Matthew's Gospel who dropped everything to follow Jesus when they were called. That is how I felt. I am not sure how they felt about being called, but I felt blessed to be called to do what I was doing.

Ignatian Spirituality invites us to find God in all things. I found God every day in the simplicity of my new life with my mom. Never having to set an alarm clock. Wearing casual clothes every day. Reading for hours at a time for entertainment. Not worrying if I did not sleep well at night because I did not have to face the demands of a busy schedule at work the following day. Each of these I considered comforts I could not enjoy when I was working in a school, and I thanked God for them. The ability to so easily receive Holy Communion every day, with no scheduling conflicts getting in the way of it, and to accompany my mom in doing so, was a luxury. The necessity to focus on my mom's needs in small things like where to go for lunch or in large things like how to care for her after a fall forced me to look outside myself. I thanked God for not letting me think only about my own needs. Spending more time with my cousin Patty Purcell was a blessing. Patty was in high school when she moved in with my parents, people she barely knew, after her own parents had died within a relatively short period of time. I was in college at the time and remember being moved by my parents' decision to help Patty just at the time that their own children were all out of the house. It was not an easy beginning for Patty, but as an adult she had become my parents' biggest fan. She was grateful for my parents' incredible generosity in helping her at such a vulnerable period of her life. Spending time with my niece Bridget and her family, either at a meal at her house or through their weekly visits to my mom or by transporting her kids when they needed a ride and could not yet drive themselves, allowed me to get to know all of them so much better than I would have if I had been living my professional life in Chicago. This was particularly meaningful because both Bridget and her daughter Grace are my goddaughters. I thanked God for the extra time I spent with them. I saw God in each of these aspects of my time with my mom.

The grace with which my mother accepted her dependency on me was amazing. She often said that my father's time in Korea prepared her for the time in her life after his death. When my parents had three young children, my father served as a medic in the Korean War. For the two years he was away, my mom and the children lived with her parents. My older siblings have fond memories of living on the farm. My mom expressed nothing but gratitude for her parents and the help they provided her at that time. But she also expressed how difficult it was to be without her husband for those two years. I believe that just as she had to depend upon her parents in my dad's absence, she also had to depend on me after his death. After all, her love of more than 69 years, the one on whom she depended for so much and who depended upon her for so much, was gone. And age and dementia had stripped her of her ability to do so many things on her own. In some ways, she had no choice but to accept her dependency. But she could have done so begrudgingly. Instead, she made me feel like she was happy to have me there. I hope that the fiercely independent woman that I am can remember this when the day comes that I may need assistance!

Watching my mother's decline due to dementia over a longer period of time than I anticipated helped prepare me for my mother's death. In fact, it allowed me to begin the grief process while she was still alive. I grieved for her loss of so many capabilities. I missed my mom as I used to know her. Sometimes, people will say of someone with dementia, "She is not the same person anymore." In some ways that is true with all the changes that occur, and I know why someone would say that;

however, in other ways that could not be further from the truth. The person with dementia is the same person God created and loves, even if her earthly existence has changed. Grieving while my mom was still living only strengthened my belief that death was not the end. I did not fear death for my mom, although I certainly was sad about it. I did fear any physical discomfort that she would suffer. But I knew something grand awaited her, that her physical death would lead her into eternal life, the goal of life's journey on earth.

Overall, the experience of caring for my mom stretched me farther than I thought I could go and in ways that I did not anticipate. I am grateful for having had the experience. It made me a better person.

Dear God, help me always to have hope.

Amen.

Conclusion

"In all circumstances give thanks . . ."

1 Thessalonians 5:18

Many times throughout my caregiver experience with my mother, friends would comment that they hoped my siblings were appreciative of what I was doing. Every time, I responded that, to a person, each of my siblings thanked me regularly for taking care of our mother. Their gratitude reminded me that we were in it together for the sake of our mother.

Never did the fact that I was not alone appear as clear as when I did my 'research' for this book. As I read through hundreds of pages of text messages, I noted how often Maryl invited my mom and me to her house for dinner or for me to take a swim in her pool. She knew that any activity was good for our mother and was important to help keep me sane. I also noted how often Colleen offered helpful suggestions that came from her experience as a mother but also as one who had worked in a nursing home when she was young. In both sets of text messages, I saw how frequently we referred to laughing and to crying about what was happening with my mom.

What I can only remember but not review, since they are not recorded, are the hundreds, perhaps thousands, of phone conversations with all the members of my family. The support they showed me through inquiries about my mom, concern for my wellbeing, and mundane small talk about life – a reminder that there was life outside my concerns for my mom – is something I never took for granted and will always remember.

I laughed and cried as I wrote this book, for the memories both happy and sad of my mom, and for the fact that the most noble work I have done in my life – noble not because of how I did it but because of what my mother needed – was for a brief three years and is behind me. If you are caring for someone with dementia, or if you know someone with dementia, I hope your reading my story has resonated with your experience in some way and led you to recognize the noble work before you as you journey with that person. If you do not yet know someone with dementia, chances are good that you will sometime in your life. Buckle up! The ride can be like no other, with surprising twists, turns, and bumps, as well as countless blessings.

Dear God, thank you for the love and support

of my family that allowed us to offer our

mother the best we could until her death.

Amen.

www.ingramcontent.com/pod-product-compliance
Lightning Source LLC
Chambersburg PA
CBHW031552040426

42452CB00006B/287